LET'S LOOK AT COUNTRIES

D0809653

LET'S LOOK AT
COLOMBIA

BY MARY BOONE

DISCARD

CAPSTONE PRESS
a capstone imprint

Pebble Plus is published by Capstone Press,
1710 Roe Crest Drive, North Mankato, Minnesota 56003
www.mycapstone.com

Library of Congress Cataloging-in-Publication Data
Names: Boone, Mary, 1963- author.
Title: Let's look at Colombia/by Mary Boone.
Description: North Mankato, Minnesota: Pebble, a Capstone imprint, 2020.
Series: Pebble Plus. Let's Look at Countries | Audience: K to grade 3. Audience: Ages 5-7.
Identifiers: LCCN 2019002056| ISBN 9781543572063 (hardcover) | ISBN 9781543574708 (pbk.) |
ISBN 9781543572223 (ebook pdf)
Subjects: LCSH: Colombia—Juvenile literature.
Classification: LCC F2258.5 .B66 2020 | DDC 986.1—dc23
LC record available at https://lccn.loc.gov/2019002056

Editorial Credits
Jessica Server, editor; Juliette Peters, designer; Jo Miller, media researcher;
Laura Manthe, production specialist

Photo Credits
Shutterstock: Carmela Soto, Cover Bottom, Cover Back, Christian Musat, 8, EGT-1, 11, F. A.
Alba, 4-5, Globe Turner, 22 (Inset), Inspired By Maps, 1, javarman, 6-7, Jess Kraft, 22-23, 24,
Mikadun, Cover Top, nale, 4 (map), nehophoto, 13, Ondrej Prosicky, Cover Middle, oscarhdez, 16,
OSTILL is Franck Camhi, 15, Pototskiy, 18-19, Simon Pittet, 17, streetflash, 2-3, sunsinger, 20-21,
TravelStrategy, 9

All internet sites appearing in back matter were available and accurate when this book
was sent to press.

Note to Parents and Teachers

The Let's Look at Countries set supports national curriculum standards for social studies related to
people, places, and culture. This book describes and illustrates Colombia. The images support early
readers in understanding the text. The repetition of words and phrases helps early readers learn
new words. This book also introduces early readers to subject-specific vocabulary words, which are
defined in the Glossary section. Early readers may need assistance to read some words and to use
the Table of Contents, Glossary, Read More, Internet Sites, Critical Thinking Questions, and Index
sections of the book.

Printed and bound in China.
1654

TABLE OF CONTENTS

Where Is Colombia?

Colombia is in South America. It is three times larger than the U.S. state of California. Colombia's capital is Bogotá.

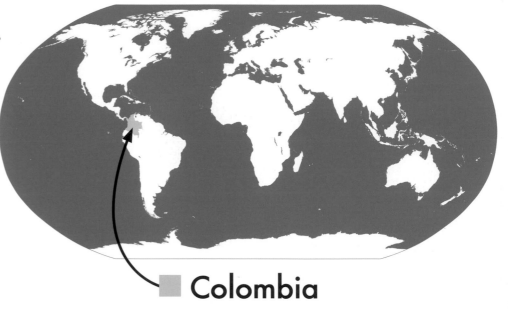

Colombia

Bogotá

From Mountains to Beaches

The Andes Mountains are one part of Colombia's landscape. Beaches line the north and west. Grasslands grow in the eastern part of the country. The Amazon Rain Forest is in the south.

In the Wild

Many animals live in Colombia. The Andean condor is the national bird. The spectacled bear lives in forests. It is South America's only bear.

spectacled bear

Andean condor

People

American Indians have lived in Colombia for thousands of years. Others came to the country from Europe or Africa. Today Spanish is Colombia's official language.

At the Table

Arepas are flat, round patties of corn flour. People eat them with cheese or eggs. Colombians also eat a chicken and potato soup called *ajiaco*.

arepas

Festivals

Carnaval de Barranquilla is Colombia's largest celebration. It happens every year before Lent. The festival includes costumes, music, parades, and dancing.

On the Job

Many Colombians have jobs that help others. They are teachers, nurses, or bus drivers. Some work in markets. Others are farmers or shipbuilders.

Transportation

Airplanes fly people over Colombia's mountains and forests. In cities Colombians use taxis and cars. People travel between cities in buses and vans called *colectivos*.

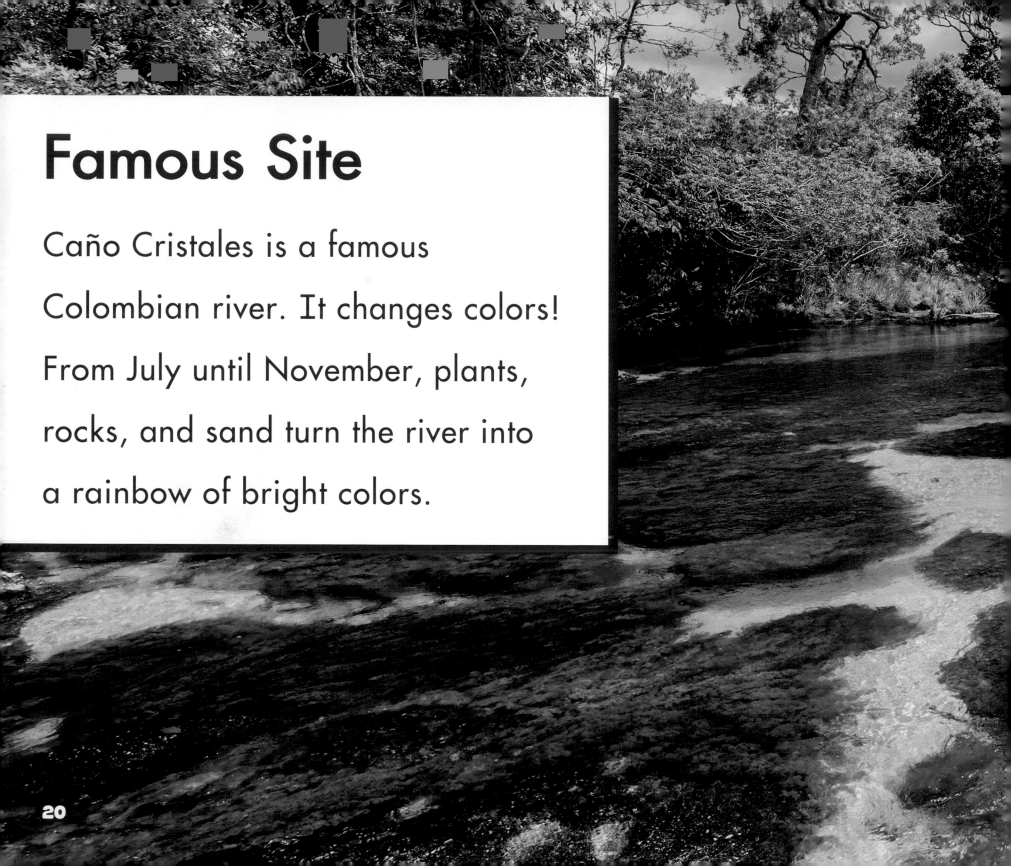

Famous Site

Caño Cristales is a famous Colombian river. It changes colors! From July until November, plants, rocks, and sand turn the river into a rainbow of bright colors.

COLOMBIA QUICK FACTS

Colombia's flag

Name: Colombia

Capital: Bogotá

Other major cities: Barranquilla, Cali, Cartagena, and Medellin

Population: 49.6 million (November 2018 estimate)

Size: 428,380 square miles (1,109,500 sq km)

Language: Spanish

Money: Colombian peso

GLOSSARY

capital—the city in a country where the government is based

celebration—a special gathering

grassland—a large area of wild grasses

Lent—the 40 days during which Christians prepare for Easter

official—approved by those in authority

patty—a small, flat cake of chopped food

rain forest—a thick forest where rain falls almost every day

READ MORE

Markovics, Joyce L. *Colombia.* Countries We Come From. New York: Bearport Publishing, 2016.

Oachs, Emily Rose. *South America.* Discover the Continents. Minneapolis: Bellwether Media, Inc., 2016.

Wiseman, Blaine. *Colombia.* Exploring Countries. New York: Smartbook Media Inc., 2018.

INTERNET SITES

National Geographic Kids: Colombia
https://kids.nationalgeographic.com/explore/countries/colombia/#colombia-dancing.jpg

Science Kids: Colombia Facts for Kids
http://www.sciencekids.co.nz/sciencefacts/countries/colombia.html

CRITICAL THINKING QUESTIONS

1. Describe some of the landforms found in Colombia.

2. If you visited Colombia, what would you like to do or see?

3. What makes Colombia different from where you live?

INDEX

5